THIS BOOK WAS DONATED BY

WEST DAKOTA WATER LLC

Drawing Is Awesome!

DRAWING AWESOME
FARM ANIMALS

Damien Toll

WINDMILL
BOOKS

Contents

Introduction

Drawing is a fun and rewarding hobby for children and adults alike. This book is designed to show how easy it is to draw great pictures by building them in simple stages.

What you will need

Only basic materials are required for effective drawing. These are:

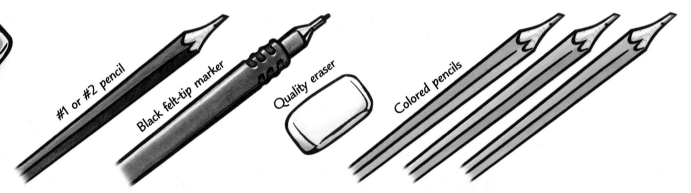

#1 or #2 pencil   Black felt-tip marker   Quality eraser   Colored pencils

These will be enough to get started. Avoid buying the cheapest pencils. Their leads often break off in the sharpener, even before they can be used. The leads are also generally too hard, making them difficult to see on the page.

Cheap erasers also cause problems by smudging rather than erasing. This often leaves a permanent stain on the paper. By spending a little more on art supplies in these areas, problems such as these can be avoided.

When purchasing a black marker, choose one to suit the size of your drawings. If you draw on a large scale, a thick felt-tip marker may be necessary. If you draw on a medium scale, a medium-point marker will do and if on a small scale, a 0.3 mm, 0.5 mm, 0.7 mm, or 0.8 mm felt-tip marker will work best.

The Stages

Simply follow the lines drawn in orange on each stage using your #1 or #2 pencil. The blue lines on each stage show what has already been drawn in the previous stages.

1.

2.

3.

In the final stage the drawing has been outlined in black and the simple shape and wire frame lines erased. The shapes are only there to help us build the picture. We finish the picture by drawing over the parts we need to make it look like our subject with the black marker, and then erasing all the simple shape lines.

Included here is a sketch of the rabbit as it would be originally drawn by an artist.

4.

These are how all the animals in this book were originally worked out and drawn. The orange and blue stages you see above are just a simplified version of this process. The drawing here has been made by many quick pencil strokes working over each other to make the line curve smoothly. It does not matter how messy it is as long as the artist knows the general direction of the line to follow with the black marker at the end. The pencil lines are erased and a clean outline is left. Therefore, do not be afraid to make a little mess with your #1 or #2 pencil, as long as you do not press so hard that you cannot erase it afterwards.

5.

Grids made of squares are set behind each stage in this book. Make sure to draw a grid lightly on your page so it does not press into the paper and show up after being erased. Artist tips have also been added to show you some simple things that can make your drawing look great. Have fun!

The Cow

Cows are females. They are big creatures that spend most of the day eating grass. That's a lot of grass, so they have four stomachs to put it all in. When they are not eating they are generally resting. There are many types of cows. Some cows are bred to produce milk to make dairy products and some cows are bred for meat.

1.

Draw a grid with four equal squares going across and three down.

Look to see where the shapes are located on the grid. Draw your head and body shapes in the same positions and draw a small line between the head and body.

Check you have drawn the correct shape and it is in the right position on the grid before going onto the next stage.

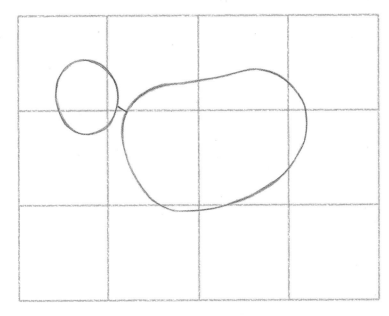

2.

Here we add more simple shapes for the horns, snout, and udder. The legs are drawn in as wire frames at first. This shows us where to draw around them to fill them in later.

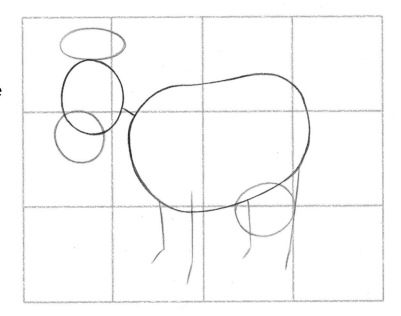

3.

Once the basic shapes have been put in, details can be added. Here the eyes, nose, and mouth have been drawn inside the existing head and nose shapes. The ears, horns, neck, tail, and hips are drawn onto the basic shapes. Notice how the legs and feet are drawn directly over the top of the wire frame legs.

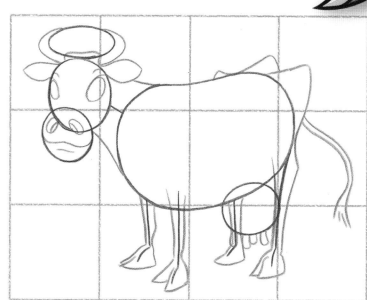

Artist Tip:

Notice the lighting and shading on the body. Light wraps around the objects. The snout, face, body, and udder all have light on their undersides.

Just above that light is some shading. Anywhere light does not hit will be shaded. The inside of the leg is a good example of this.

4.

This is a lazy dairy cow. Lowering the eyelids over her eyes gives her a lazy expression.

Add some grass and maybe even a mountain range in the background to finish the scene.

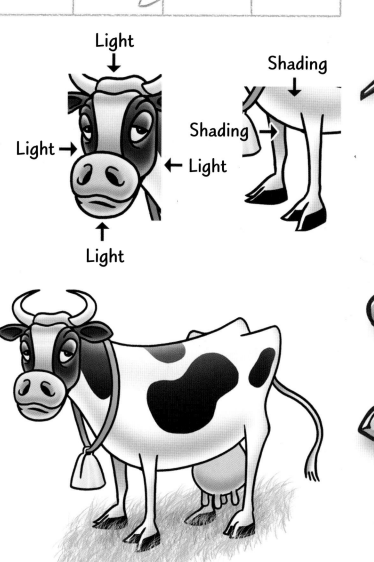

The Donkey

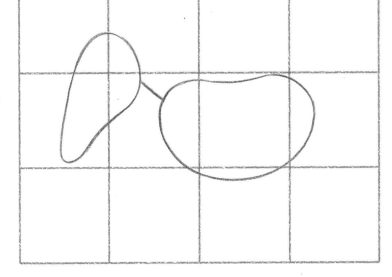

Donkeys are related to horses and zebras. They are smaller than horses and make a "hee-haw" sound. A lifespan of around 30 to 50 years makes them one of the longest-living animals on Earth. People have used donkeys for thousands of years to carry and pull things.

1.

Draw a grid with four equal squares going across and three down.

You will notice most of the pictures begin the same way with drawing the basic shape for the body and head first. Join the head and body with a wire frame for the neck.

2.

Draw in the facial features. Add the ears and the top of the donkey's head and neck.

Wire frame legs are used and we build the legs around these. Draw the donkey's hooves at the bottom of the legs.

3.

Add in the legs over the wire frames. Put in the tail and finish off with the last of the facial features.

Artist Tip:

Expression gives life to a drawing. The eyes and the mouth are the key areas for this. We use human expression because we can relate to that feeling. Here are some other expressions you may like to try.

Happy   Laughing   Fright   Angry

4.

This donkey's expression is stubborn. Donkeys have often been thought of as being stubborn animals. Although this may not be true, the stereotype of the stubborn mule (another name for a donkey) lives on.

The Dog

Dogs are known as "man's best friend." These intelligent animals can be trained to perform many tasks. On cattle and sheep farms they round up livestock and can herd them from one paddock to another. The farmer will often use a whistle to communicate to the dog where he wants it to go.

1.

Draw a grid with four equal squares going across and three down.

Again we draw in the body and head first using basic shapes.
As with all the basic shapes in this book, try to imagine these shapes being 3-D.

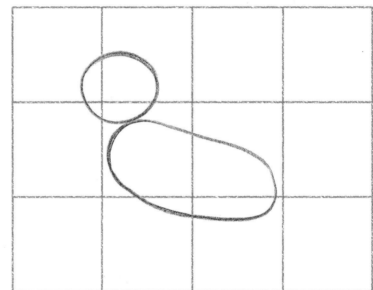

2.

Add the ears, the top of the head, and the snout.

The tail and the legs are wire frames to show which direction they are pointing.

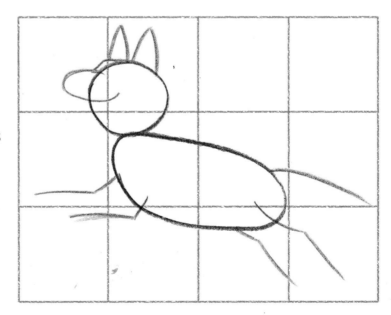

3.

Draw in the neck and mouth. Add the eye at the top of the head shape and a nose on the snout.

Then draw the legs and tail around the wire frames.

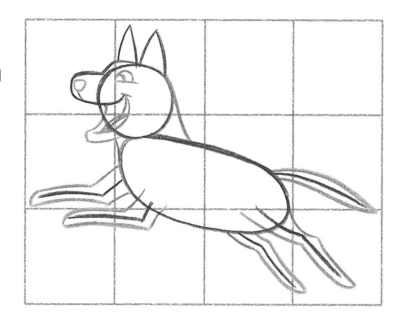

4.

Finish the picture with some color. Here we have put in a fence that the dog is jumping over. You may like to put in something else. You could draw in the sheep that appears later in this book.

The Sheep

Like cows, sheep spend most of their day grazing. They stay together in a group called a flock. They have poor eyesight but great hearing. Male sheep are called rams, females are called ewes, and babies are called lambs. Sheep have a fluffy white coat which is called wool. Once a year they are shorn for this wool which is then used to make clothes.

1.

Draw a grid with four equal squares going across and three down.

Draw in the shapes for the body and head in the right positions on the grid.

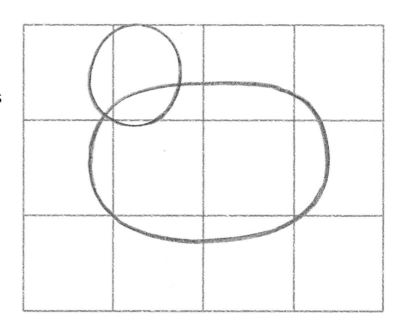

2.

Draw in the snout, mouth and some of the facial features. Add the wire frame legs.

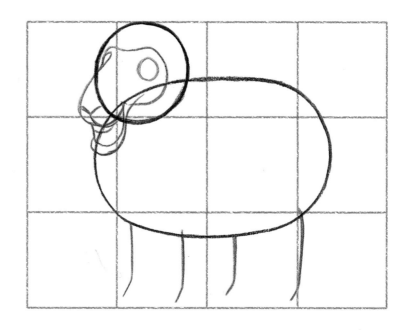

3.

The wool is drawn around the body shape in bumps. Draw the legs over the wire frames.

Draw eyebrows, ears and pupils in the eyes.

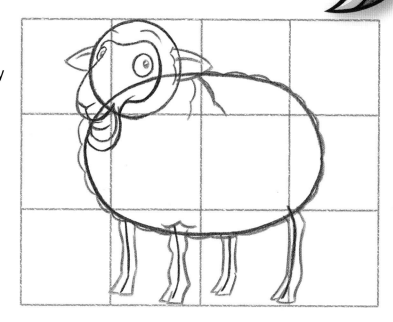

Artist Tip:

When using a felt-tip marker try to apply light pressure at the beginning of the line, then press down a little firmer as you go along the line. Gradually reduce the pressure when coming to the end of the line. This will give you a varied line width that can look quite effective. Notice how the lines go to points.

If using a larger marker, don't leave it in the same place on the paper. If you do this it will leave a big round ugly dot.

Pointed ends from releasing pressure at end of line.

4.

Even though sheep are white, a light blue can be used for shading. Could this be the sheep the dog is jumping over on page 9?

Cartoon Sheep

Sheep are known for their wool. Grandmas are often known for knitting wool sweaters while relaxing in rocking chairs. Here we have combined the two to come up with a sweater made directly from the wool source; a cartoon Grandma sheep. How about ewe trying it!

1.

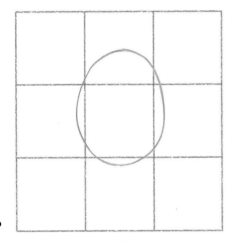

Draw a square grid with three equal squares going across and down.

Begin with the simple body shape on the grid.

2.

Add the circle for the head and wire frame arms with circles on the ends. Draw in the shape for the lap and wire frame legs and feet.

3.

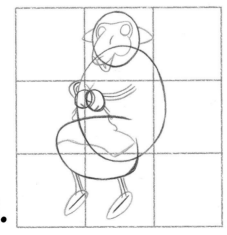

Draw in the face, ears, arms, and legs. Define the hands inside the circles and draw a stretched egg shape for the slippers on the feet. Add in the knitting and the knitting needles.

4.

Remember to only draw the lines needed to finish the picture. Most of the lines are only guidelines that will be rubbed out.

The Rooster

Roosters are male chickens. They are well known for their loud announcements of "cock-a-doodle-doo!" at dawn. Roosters do not get along well with other roosters and will fight to establish their dominance. For this reason there is usually only one rooster allowed in every coop of chickens.

1.

Draw a grid with two equal squares going across and three down.

Draw in the body shape and the wire-frame legs and feet.

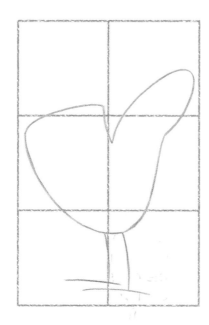

2.

Add a shape for the head, and the crest atop the head. Draw on some basic shapes for the arms and add in the toes.

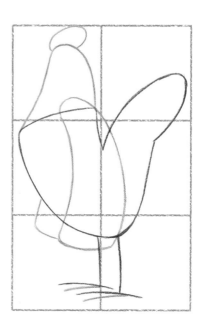

3.

Facial features can now be added and the body can be defined within the basic shapes. Draw in the face, feet, and hands and define the tail feathers.

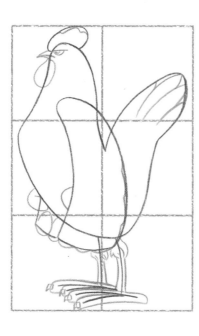

4.

Color in the rooster to finish.

The Chicken

Chickens are very common on farms. At birth, they are bright yellow and known as chicks. In their first year they are called pullets and after that they are known as hens. Although they have wings, chickens cannot fly very far. Chickens lay eggs. If these eggs are sat on by the chickens long enough, they will hatch, revealing a baby chick.

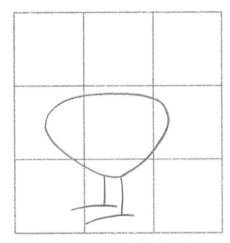

1. Draw a square grid with three equal squares going across and down.

Begin with a triangular shape for the body. Add wire frame legs and feet.

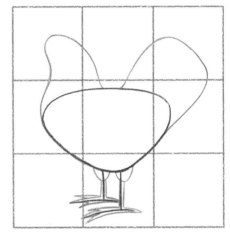

2. Draw the shape for the neck and head. Add the shape for the tail. Draw the legs and feet around the wire frames, adding a couple of extra toes on the feet.

3. Draw in the facial features. Draw a sideways "C" for the wing and separate the tail into feathers.

4. Outline your chicken, erase the pencil lines, and color it in.

Cartoon Chicken

Young chickens are called chicks. Adult male chickens are called roosters and adult female chickens are called hens. Here we have exaggerated the female characteristics of the hen by giving her items usually associated with women. The dress and the handbag give her a feminine character which helps us imagine her as very motherly.

1.

Draw a grid with two equal squares going across and three down.

First draw an oblong looking-oval. This is the chicken's body.

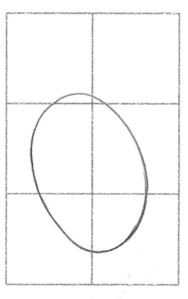

2.

Add shapes for the head and tail. The arm is a jelly-bean shape. Draw in the skirt bottoms and the wire-frame legs and feet.

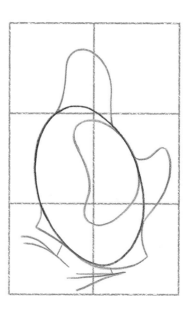

3.

Add the beak, comb, and the other facial features. Draw in the frills on the dress neck and arms. Fill in the legs and feet.

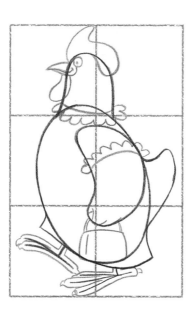

4.

Add some flowers to the dress, erase the pencil lines and color it in.

The Duck

Ducks spend most of their time on water. They have wide, flat bodies covered in waterproof feathers that enable them to float very well. Webbed feet allow them to paddle around with ease in the water. They are also well known for flying. Ducks can fly great distances to escape severe cold temperatures. Let's draw two different ducks!

1.

Draw a square grid with three squares going across and down.

After the body and head have been drawn in, a long wire frame neck has been added. This makes it much easier to show where the neck will be positioned.

Complete the picture following the orange shapes and lines on each stage. When the duck is outlined, rub out the shapes and color.

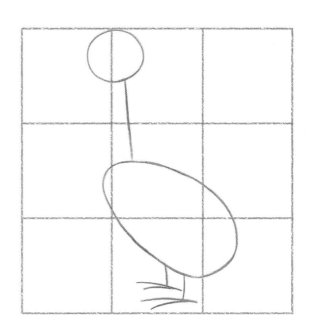

2.

3.

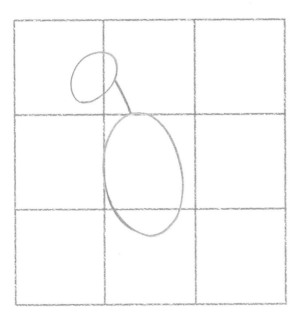

1.

Draw a square grid with three squares going across and down. Draw in the body first, then the head and wire frame.

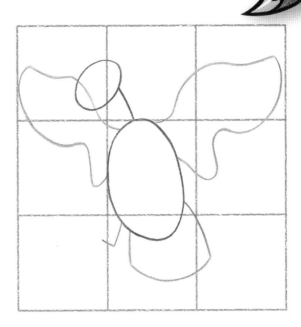

2.

Add the shapes for the wings and tail, and a wire frame leg.

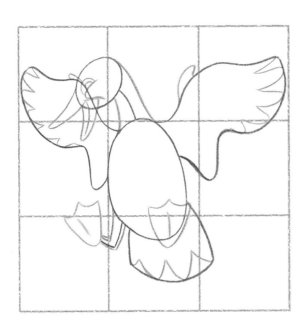

3.

Define the features in the wings and tail. Add the face and neck. Draw in the feet and the leg surrounding the wire frame.

4.

Color the duck, not forgetting to add shading to the parts blocked out by the sun such as the feet and stomach.

Crouching Dog

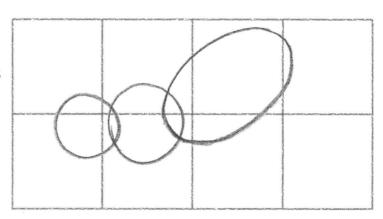

Here we have a dog in a herding position. The dog will lower its head and stare the herd in the eye, showing dominance. Once the dog gains dominance of the herd, it can guide it where the farmer wants it to go. It is in this way that the dogs are of real value to farmers.

1.

Draw a grid with four equal squares going across and two down.

Draw in the three basic shapes making up the body and head.

2.

Add the wire frame legs and tail. The muscle on the back leg has also been drawn as a basic shape.

3.

Draw the head, facial features, and ears over the basic shape at the front. Connect the shapes together with lines merging onto the shapes. Go around the wire-frame legs and tail, and draw in the paws.

Artist Tip:

All the eyes in this book have a little white on them. This is called a highlight. Anything that is wet or has a smooth surface will reflect light making a highlight. The dog's nose also has a highlight. This simple technique brings life to a drawing. Add a highlight by simply not coloring in part of the eye or nose around the top of it.

4.

You could draw the dog staring at the sheep in this book or maybe a cow or bull. How about putting in a background of a distant fence with grass all around showing the dog working in a paddock.

The Bull

A bull is a male cow. They are much more muscular than cows and have thicker legs. Bulls can be aggressive and have a lot of weight to throw around if they want to. They will charge if provoked. Like cows, they spend most of their day eating grass or otherwise resting.

1.

Draw a grid with four equal squares going across and three down.

First draw in the basic shape for the body.

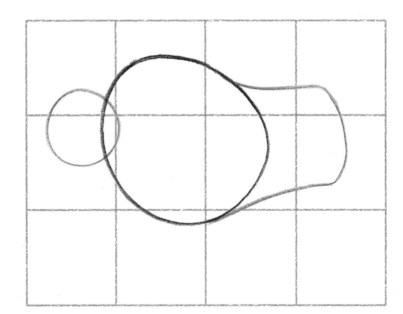

2.

Add the shape for the head and a squarish shape for the rear of the animal.

3.

Add a circle that will become the nose and mouth. Put in wire frames for the legs and a kinked tail.

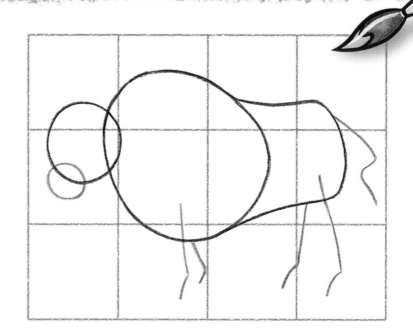

4.

Draw in the face, ears, and horns and connect the bottom of the face to the basic body shape.

Draw thick legs around the wire frames and a tail with a frayed end. Add the finishing features of the hip at the top of the rear and the hanging belly.

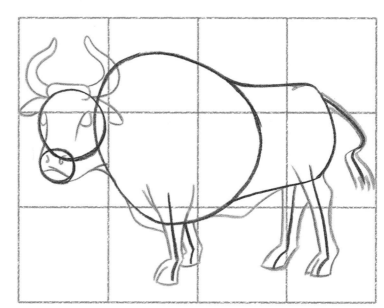

5.

Notice the light surrounding the animal. Refer to the artist tip for the cow earlier.

The Pig

Pigs are large-bodied animals with big heads and a prominent snout. The snout is used to turn over soil when looking for food. Pigs are known to be intelligent, and stay cool by rolling in mud and water. They are thought to be so sensitive that you can actually hurt their feelings.

1.

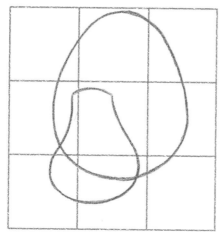

Draw a square grid with three equal squares going across and down.

Begin with a large shape for the body and a pear shape for the head.

2.

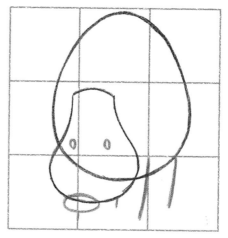

Draw an oval under the pear. Add some eyes in the middle of the pear. Draw in the wire frames for the legs.

3.

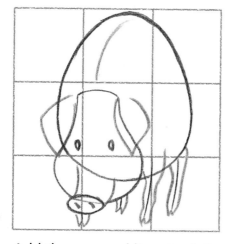

Add the ears and lines to define the snout. Draw the legs around the wire frames and a line down the center of the back.

4.

Outline your drawing and erase the pencil lines. Color your pig.

Cartoon Pig

A pig's favorite pastime is eating. Making a cartoon character of a pig about to eat a big meal seems only natural. To make it fun we have given him a knife and fork and made him upright, like a human. By adding human features and expressions we can relate to our character, making it as if we can understand how they feel.

1.

Draw a grid with two equal squares going across and three down.

This shape starts like a warped egg.

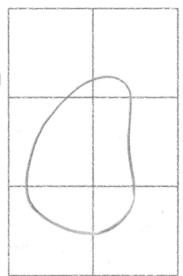

2.

Add a basic shape for the head and back legs. Wireframe arms and feet complete this stage.

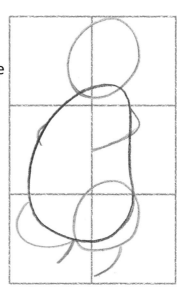

3.

Add the snout, facial features, and ears. Draw the arms and feet over the wire frames, making sure to slit the ends for the hooves.

4.

Add a table with some food and a knife and fork. Erase the pencil lines and color.

The Rabbit

Rabbits are small furry creatures that live underground in a home called a warren. The tunnels that lead to these warrens are called burrows. Female rabbits can give birth to 30 or 40 babies each year. A group of rabbits is called a herd. Rabbits come to the surface in the morning and at dusk to feed on the grass.

1.

Draw a grid with four equal squares going across and three down.

The body shape resembles an egg on its side. Draw this low on the grid.

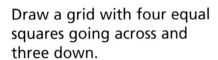

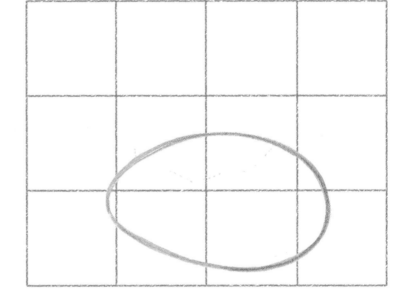

2.

Add the head shape which also looks like an egg. The back leg is represented with a basic shape. Draw in the semicircle tail and the wire frame legs.

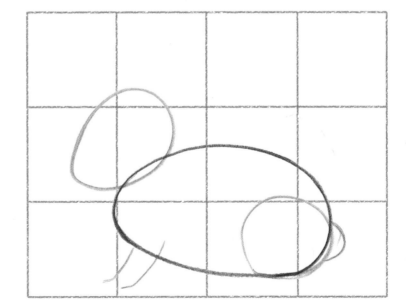

24

3.

Add on the ears and draw around the wire frame legs. Add the back foot and finish this stage with the "V" nose, cheeks, and eye.

Artist Tip:

To draw whiskers, hair and grass, place your pencil on the paper as you would normally to draw. Flick your pencil while curving it slightly. Repeat this process in a random pattern to fill in the area.

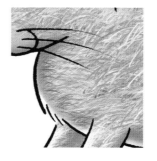

4.

Remember to leave some of the eye white for a highlight. When the outline is finished and the pencil lines rubbed out, add the whiskers on the cheeks.

Cartoon Rabbit

Many cartoon characters are made to stand tall and act like humans. By combining the speed of the rabbit with the features of a human we create a cartoon character. Cartoon characters exaggerate their talents, and what better feature to exaggerate on a rabbit than its speed? Rabbits can reach over 35 miles per hour (55 kilometers per hour).

1.

Draw a grid with four equal squares going across and three down.

This drawing is started with an action line, which is what the drawing is centered on. In this drawing the rabbit has a lean so the action line shows the extent of that lean.

The body and head shapes are placed over the action line.

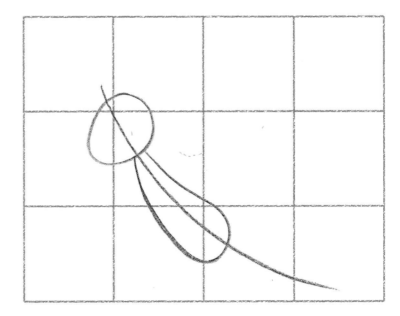

2.

An oval has been added for the legs and a circle for the tail. The feet and the arms are wire framed. At the end of the arms are circles which will encase the hands.

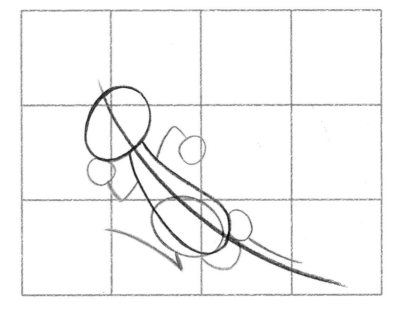

3.

Define the face within the shortened egg and add the ears. Draw around the wire frame arms and define the hands inside and slightly out of the circles.

Draw in the feet. There is a line outside the grid which will be a shadow on the ground.

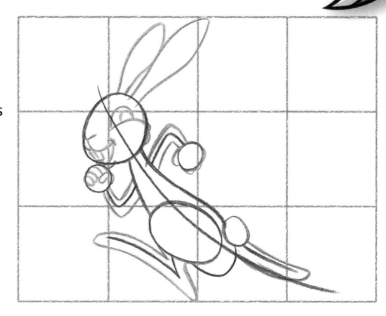

Artist Tip:

A few lines and a puff of dust behind the character suggests speed. A shadow underneath is important as it shows that the character is off the ground in full flight.

4.

Outline your drawing and erase the pencil lines. Rabbits come in many different colors and coat patterns. You could experiment with these and come up with your own new breed of cartoon speedy rabbit.

The Horse

The horse has been our working and traveling companion for thousands of years. They were used for pulling chariots in ancient times and carriages in more recent times. On farms they would be used to plow fields. Today, horses are mainly used for show, recreation, and racing purposes. There are, however, parts of the world where wild horses still roam.

1.

Draw a grid with four equal squares going across and three down.

Start with what looks like a warped jelly bean. This is the horse's body.

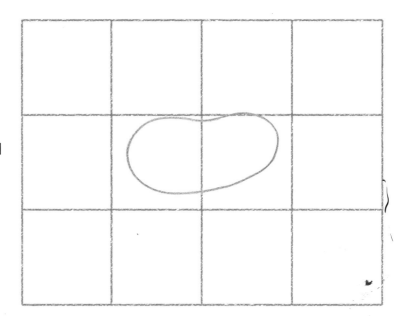

2.

Add the wire frame legs and tail. The wire frame shows where the bends are.

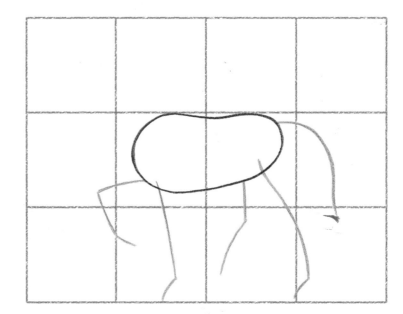

3.

Draw in the neck, mane, and head. Add a bushy tail over the wire frame.

4.

Fill in the details of the head and mane, and draw in the legs and hooves.

5.

Remember to shade the inside of the legs and under the neck, belly and tail. Leave the edges where the light shines a lighter shade.

Cartoon Horse

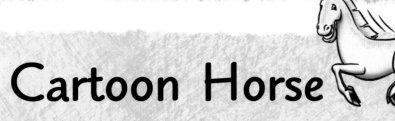

Horse shows involve a lot of jumping and horses can jump very high. What better way to draw a cartoon of a horse than to have it bounding over a jumping pole? Here our horse is happily springing over the high beam with almost no effort at all. This exaggerates their ability to leap.

1.

Draw a grid with four equal squares going across and three down.

Draw in the body shape first. This looks like a flattened egg. Be careful to place it in the correct position on the grid.

Add a long shape rounded at the top and bottom for the head and a circle for the back leg.

2.

Draw in the lines for the neck and add lines for the wire frame legs and tail.

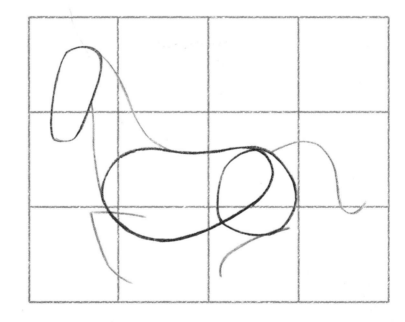

3.

Create the horse over the top of these shapes and wire frames by adding the ears, mane and facial features.

Draw in the legs. Notice how the legs on the opposite side of the horse are very similar to the legs closest to us. Draw on the tail to finish this stage.

Artist Tip:

Lines around the character can show movement. Lines on the side show it is moving in one direction.

Lines on every side would make it look like the character is shaking, as if it were cold.

4.

Even a white horse has parts where light will not reach. By carefully choosing the parts we shade, we can create a 3-D look while still keeping a white horse. You could have it jumping over a bar, or over one of the other animals in this book.

Published in 2015 by **Windmill Books,**
an Imprint of Rosen Publishing,
29 East 21st Street, New York, NY 10010.

Written and illustrated by Damien Toll.
With thanks to Jared Gow.

Library of Congress Cataloging-in-Publication Data
Toll, Damien.
  Drawing awesome farm animals / Damien Toll.
      pages cm. — (Drawing is awesome!)
  Includes index.
ISBN 978-1-4777-5462-7 (pbk.)
ISBN 978-1-4777-5488-7 (6 pack)
ISBN 978-1-4777-5469-6 (library binding)
1. Domestic animals in art—Juvenile literature.
2. Livestock in art—Juvenile literature.
3. Drawing—Technique—Juvenile literature.
I. Title.
 NC783.8.D65T65 2015
 743.6—dc23

                                          2014027090

Manufactured in the United States of America

CPSIA Compliance Information: Batch # CW15WM: For Further Information contact
Rosen Publishing, New York, New York at 1-800-237-9932